500 LESSON PLAN TIPS FOR SCHOOL TEACHERS

DR DHEERAJ MEHROTRA

Made with ❤ on the Notion Press Platform
www.notionpress.com

Contents

Preface

Teaching is an art that thrives on preparation, adaptability, and innovation. Lesson planning, at the heart of this art, serves as a blueprint for impactful learning experiences, ensuring that educators meet curriculum goals and inspire and engage their students. However, the process can often feel overwhelming, requiring a balance of creativity, structure, and practicality. **500 Lesson Plan Tips for School Teachers** *is a comprehensive guide designed to empower educators with actionable strategies, insights, and creative ideas. Whether you're a seasoned teacher refining your approach or a new educator seeking clarity, this book offers tips to enhance classroom efficiency, address diverse learner needs, and integrate technology and innovation into teaching. Each tip is curated to reflect the evolving landscape of education, emphasizing inclusivity, critical thinking, and engagement. Let us celebrate the power of education and the difference teachers make every day.*

— www.authordheerajmehrotra.com

Effective Lesson Planning for Young Learners

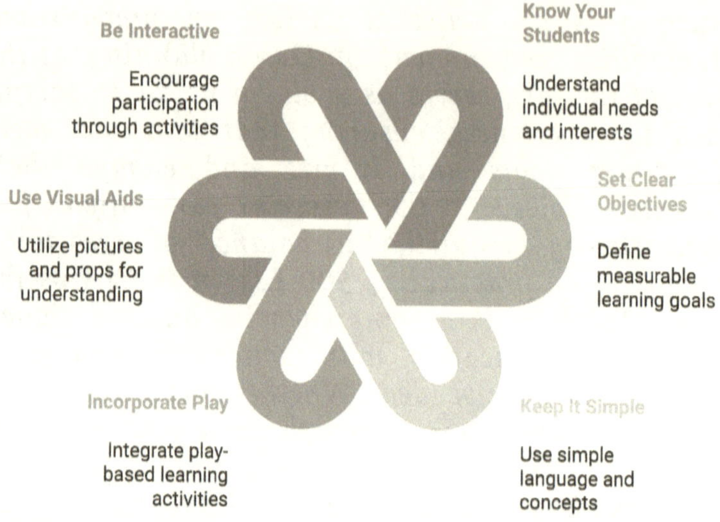

I
Effective Lesson Plan Ideas

Madeline Hunter: "A good lesson plan is the teacher's road map for creating an effective and engaging learning experience."

Foundational Concepts in Planning

Make your learning goals crystal clear.
Establish instructional objectives under the
requirements of the curriculum.
Find out how your pupils learn best.
Use backward design to plan: think about the result
first.
Make a comprehensive plan for each class.
To add depth, use Bloom's Taxonomy.
Have a good mix of content and activities.
Give reasonable deadlines.
Get backup plans ready in case anything goes wrong.
Allocate some time for students to contemplate.

❧

Grant Wiggins: "Start with the end in mind. Design lessons with clear goals that shape all instruction and assessment."

Creating Content

Include a variety of sources in your lesson plans.
Analogies can be used to simplify complicated
subjects.
Use visual aids such as graphs and charts.
Organise materials that are differentiated.
Establish connections between content and practical
uses.
Add interactive multimedia elements to pique interest.
Stack information in a progressive manner.
Ditch the data deluge.
To make lessons stick in students' minds, use stories.
Students' work should be included.

Carol Ann Tomlinson: "Lesson plans must be flexible frameworks to respond to the needs of learners."

ॐ

Methods for Engagement

Begin by posing a captivating inquiry.
Make use of topic-related warm-up exercises.
Arrange for experimental or recreational activities
that include direct physical contact.
Work in both small groups and on your own for a
change.
Incorporate game mechanics.
Make sure to incorporate breaks within your long
lessons.
To make people laugh, use the right jokes.
Tailor the content to the interests of the students.
Create activities that encourage students to answer
questions.
For a more in-depth involvement, incorporate
reflection tasks.

John Dewey: "Education is not preparation for life; education is life itself. Plan to make learning meaningful."

Resources and Tools

Visual aids such as Venn diagrams should be applied
as organisers.
Take advantage of LMSs in your teaching.
Find instructional apps that you may use for free.
Make sure to print out the handouts beforehand.
Use ChatGPT and other AI tools for your research.
Make a note of valuable movies and materials you
find online.
Utilise online educational excursions.
Always keep a supply of other plans on hand.
Make sure to revise and update all course materials
regularly.
For open and honest evaluations, use rubrics.

"Great teaching begins with great planning." – Anonymous

Planning Focused on Students

To personalise and collect student input.
Plan with the use of formative assessments.
Encourage students to teach one another.
Allow students to have a say in their work.
Facilitate adaptable educational routes.
Motivate individuals to conduct their study.
Include time for students to talk to each other.
Provide opportunities for self-evaluation.
Consider a wide range of student abilities when developing your plan.
Recognise each person's accomplishments.

"A lesson plan is a bridge between learning objectives and classroom action." – William J. Rothwell

Integrating Assessments

Create evaluations that are in line with the goals of
the class.
Toss in both interim and final tests.
Assess comprehension with the help of exit tickets.
A simple way to check progress is with quizzes.
Prepare questions for reflective writing.
Facilitate group learning through the use of peer
evaluations.
Try evaluating projects as a whole.
Use a learning portfolio to keep tabs on your
development.
Provide the results of the evaluation right away.
Maintain a balance between quantitative and
qualitative evaluations.

"Preparation is the key to unlocking a student's potential." –
Margaret Riel

Efficiency in Managing Time

Divide lessons into brief, targeted parts.
To keep track of your activities, use timers.
Preserve a buffer zone.
The class should begin and conclude promptly.
Put important goals first and ignore side subjects.
Maintain smooth transitions between tasks.
Time can be better allocated with the use of graphic timetables.
Take note of the pace and make adjustments as needed.
Give those who finish their assignments early.
Get as much done as you can without cramming.

"Teaching without a plan is like setting sail without a map." –
Richard DuFour

Working Together and Receiving Comments

Work together with your classmates to create lessons.
Consult a mentor for advice on reviewing plans.
Engage in strategy discussions with professionals in the field.
Collaboratively teach to test out new forms.
Evaluate past classes' performance.
Watch the lessons of other educators.
Communicate the lessons you've learnt to your coworkers.
Gather student opinions by administering surveys.
Make collections of shared resources.
Join communities of practice that focus on professional development.

"Well-structured lessons create well-structured minds." –
Howard Gardner

Inspiration for Lesson Plans

Play out hypothetical situations.
Incorporate components of art-based learning.
Set up discussion groups to discuss important issues.
Make tasks similar to those found in escape rooms.
Present case studies that can be analysed.
Make use of connections that span disciplines.
Use music to help students learn.
Create tailored board games for particular themes.
Work together to write stories.
Arrange for classes to be held in natural environments.

৪৩

"Lesson planning is the art of predicting how students will think and act." – Anita Woolfolk

Technological Adaptation

Learn with the use of virtual reality (VR).
For evaluations, utilise digital resources.
Discover the world of AI-powered customisation.
Arrange sessions using interactive whiteboards.
Create flexible asynchronous lessons.
Audio learners can benefit from podcasts.
Add internet message boards.
Use coding tools to enhance STEM disciplines.
Use digital dashboards to keep tabs on your progress.
Make plans to educate people about cybersecurity.

"Effective education is 90% preparation, 10% execution." –
Anonymous

SEL and Embracing Change

Arrange events that highlight the importance of emotional intelligence.
Set up a time for practising mindfulness.
Embrace a wide range of cultures through the use of inclusive resources.
All learners should be able to access the content easily.
Lessons should incorporate anti-bullying elements.
Incorporate activities that foster trust amongst participants.
When speaking, avoid using terms that are specific to one gender.
Think about ways to make technology more accessible.
Mark the occasion of international days and events.
Utilise tasks that are driven by empathy.

"An organized lesson is the foundation of meaningful learning."
– Robert Marzano

Tips for Advanced Planning

Plan projects that involve many disciplines.
Make use of methods for backward mapping.
Create instruction plans that may be used again and again.
Prepare flexible lesson plans to address unexpected obstacles.
Maintain a supply of "ready-to-go" mini-lessons.
Incorporate seasonal themes to maintain the interest of students.
Highlight tasks that require solving problems.
Designate areas for quiet reading or study.
Make strategic use of humour to foster connections.
Create mnemonics that aid in memorisation.

"Failing to prepare is preparing to fail—especially in education."
– Benjamin Franklin (adapted)

SEL and Inclusivity

Promote classroom cultural exchanges.
Create diverse-inclusive games.
Include scenarios that encourage people to be socially responsible.
Acquaint readers with SEL books and media.
Plan "buddy" initiatives to help people assist each other.
Arrange events that encourage the development of empathy employing narrative.
Gather your group together to talk about fairness and equity.
Make sure to include inclusive activities throughout holidays and festivals.
Use focused educational initiatives to combat bias.
Offer content in multiple languages to help overcome language obstacles.

"Lesson plans turn aspirations into achievements." – Charlotte Danielson

Further Suggestions for Advanced Planning

Arrange field tours to various industries or museums.
Incorporate lessons on critical thinking using case studies.
Set up classes for creative writing.
Consider incorporating themed weeks, such as STEM Week.
Make problems or tests that relate to the lessons covered in the program.
Create models with practical uses in mind.
For challenging subjects, try using concept-mapping activities.
Create learning modules that are focused on projects.
Arrange that specialists be available for frequent "ask me anything" sessions.
To enhance participation, use historical role-playing.

"Engagement begins with a thoughtfully crafted lesson." – Jim Knight

Planning for Sustainability

Environmentally friendly plan lessons.
Discuss several aspects of renewable energy.
Please make plans to teach students how to limit their trash.
Promote art initiatives that involved upcycling.
Encourage eco-friendly teaching methods, such as using digital worksheets.
Come and talk about the environmental problems that the world is facing.
A green project or garden could be included.
Provide examples of local sustainability success stories or individuals who have had a significant impact.
Set up community drives, such as days to clean up trash.
Draw inspiration from the Sustainable Development Goals (SDGs).

"Your plan today shapes their future tomorrow." – Anonymous

Integrating Different Academic Fields

Science and history can be blended to create timelines of innovations.
Interpret literature through the medium of art.
Make use of mathematics in all of your budgeting endeavours.
Incorporate discussions of past innovations into the STEM curriculum.
Combine geographical research with environmental science.
Make economics a part of the social science curriculum.
Arrange classes based on significant historical relics.
Build narrative applications by integrating code with creative writing.
Add physical exercise to scientific research.
Introduce mathematical or historical patterns using music.

ಚ

"Detailed plans empower teachers to adapt creatively." – Carol Ann Tomlinson

Integration of Technology (Periodic)

Dedicate some time to learning about 3D printing and how it may be applied to STEM projects.
Make use of AR to learn in an immersive environment.
Introduce students to computational thinking through hosting coding challenges.
Tap into the power of cloud platforms to facilitate teamwork.
Try out Canva and other digital storytelling tools.
Use tools like Kahoot to create your quizzes and games.
Arrange virtual laboratories for scalable, risk-free scientific investigations.
Host hackathons to encourage innovative approaches to solving problems.
Adaptive quizzes and progress tracking can be enhanced with AI.
Organise webinars with international speakers.

"Every minute spent planning is an investment in success." –
James Clear

Techniques for Maintaining Order in the Classroom

Include cues for paying attention, such as claps or phrases.
Make time each week for students and teachers to check in with each other.
Make schedules more precise by using colour coding.
Optimise engagement by designing seating designs.
Switch up who's in charge of the classroom.
Create programs that reward people for taking part.
Develop ground rules for the classroom as a group.
Use surveys as "pulse checks" regularly.
Make better use of your time by using visual timers.
Make sure that you move between chores with care.

"The best teachers teach from the head and the heart, but also from a plan." – Lee Shulman

Learning Exercises

*"Genius hour" initiatives should be planned.
Motivate students to take part in academic
competitions.
For inspiration, watch TED Talks.
Create lesson-based community service projects.
Arrange tutoring sessions for students of different
ages.
Incorporate timed quizzes to test memorisation.
Sustain debate teams that focus on international
affairs.
Gather your creative friends for some do-it-yourself
creating.
To learn more about potential job paths, employ the
"mystery guests" technique.
Create reflective diaries monthly.*

☙

"Consistency in planning leads to consistency in results." – Doug Lemov

Maintaining Your Health as a New Teacher

Plan to deal with stress.
Leave room in your schedule for self-directed study
when you map out your goals.
Make arrangements for group sessions to provide
feedback.
Increase productivity with the help of planning
software
Update your long-term objectives frequently.
Share in the joy of team members' achievements.
To develop, look for mentorship programs.
Make flexibility a priority and avoid overplanning.
Make sure that your plans include humour and joy.
Every week, take stock of your accomplishments and
failures.

৪৩

"Plans are nothing, but planning is everything." – Dwight D. Eisenhower (adapted)

ೞ

Teacher Professional Development

*It is recommended that you participate in both
regional and international conferences.
Set up sessions where you may observe each other
working to find out what works.
Establish a reading group devoted to pedagogical
texts.
Join online seminars centred on cutting-edge teaching
methods.
I seek credentials in artificial intelligence (AI) and
educational technology (EDTech).
Hold workshops that are tailored to specific subjects to
improve skills.
Inspire your team to conduct action research.
To gain instructional insights, organise reflective
journaling sessions.
Organise guest talks by industry leaders on current
developments in education.
The academic community should institute mentorship
programs.*

ಎಲ

"Lesson planning translates theory into practice." – Grant Wiggins

❦

Implementing SEL (Social and Emotional Learning)

Develop mindfulness activities that instructors and students can do together.
Journaling can be a valuable method for processing emotions.
Carry out role-playing exercises that focus on empathy.
When doing exercises in perspective-taking, use stories.
Find ways to practise thankfulness to encourage a positive outlook.
Set up classes on how to handle conflicts.
Lead class discussions on feelings and interpersonal connections.
Develop visual tools to investigate emotions and reactions.
Work together with counsellors to put SEL objectives into action.
Create a caring learning environment by implementing restorative practices.

ಬಃ

"A lesson plan is a commitment to student growth." – John Hattie

Raising International Understanding

Create classes that address critical global issues, such as climate change.
Prompt students in foreign schools to engage in pen pal exchanges.
Discuss current events on a worldwide scale in the classroom.
Present different viewpoints from around the world through documentaries.
Honour students' diverse backgrounds by engaging them in themed classroom activities.
Share knowledge regarding the significance of languages spoken around the world.
Toss in lessons from the past that have relevance throughout the world.
Promote discussions regarding global issues such as human rights.
If you want to compare two or more economic or governmental systems, use case studies.
Collaborate across disciplines to tackle pressing global problems.

౭౩

"The magic in teaching lies in the preparation." – Anonymous

Parents' Role in Lesson Preparation

Set up sessions where students and parents can study together.
Find out what parents think about the curriculum's applicability.
Hold seminars where parents can discover efficient methods of education.
Consult with parents to ensure that lesson goals are aligned.
Make arrangements for parent-teacher conferences.
Plan a survey to gather input from parents every month.
Professionals who work with parents should be invited to talk.
Work together with parents on extracurricular activities.
Collaboratively organise educational activities for the entire community.
Give parents tools they can use at home to continue their education.

ॐ

"A teacher's lesson plan reflects their passion for learning." –
Debra Pickering

Digital Responsibility

Create a curriculum that emphasises the importance of practising safe internet habits.
Incorporate pursuits that investigate the consequences of digital traces.
Help students recognise false information and verify claims made online.
Include conversations around the ethical use of technology.
Arrange group projects that make use of online technologies for collaboration.
Dive into AI's impact on today's classrooms and communities.
Provide students with a foundational understanding of cybersecurity concepts.
Talk about proper online conduct when interacting with others online.
Establish a committee on digital citizenship and have students serve as its leaders.
Gamification is used to teach appropriate tech usage.

"Preparation inspires confidence in both teachers and learners."
– Anonymous

Evaluations and Criticisms

To measure continuous understanding, organise formative assessments.
Develop rubrics for peer evaluation of group work.
To encourage contemplation, set up self-evaluation tasks.
For immediate feedback after a lesson, utilise exit tickets.
Use interactive quizzes to get your findings right away.
Create assessments that are based on criteria to ensure uniformity.
Make sure to maintain regular student-teacher feedback conferences.
Make use of narratives to comprehend practical uses.
One way to provide feedback is through reflective journaling.
Take a look at several forms of multimedia assessment.
Please let me know if you would like anything additional!

৵

"Lesson plans ensure every learner finds their moment to shine."
– Anonymous

Advanced Methods of Instruction

Investigate blended learning models that integrate digital and conventional approaches.
Implementing flipped classes can lead to more interactive discussions.
Make use of idea mapping to see connections in complicated subjects.
Encourage curiosity through the use of inquiry-based learning.
Employing backward design in lesson planning aims to achieve specific goals.
Use individualised lessons to meet the needs of all students.
Motivate your students even more by creating gamified lesson ideas.
Encourage group work in the classroom by having students work together to solve problems.
Integrate ideas from different fields through the use of theme-based instruction.
Make time for students to teach each other to strengthen their knowledge.

ം

"Without a plan, even the best content loses its impact." – Robert J. Marzano

Educational Technology in the Classroom

*Customise learning with the help of AI tools.
Make lessons more engaging by using interactive
whiteboards.
Arrange virtual reality or augmented reality-based
pursuits for realism.
Build multimedia assets such as films and audio
recordings.
Streamline the distribution of content by utilising
learning management systems.
Find patterns in student performance by analysing
collected data.
For instant participation, use online polls and quizzes.
Enhance your studies using educational apps.
Arrange to go on virtual field trips so students can
learn by doing.
Engage pupils in activities that promote the
appropriate use of technology.*

"Planning builds the structure; teaching adds the color." –
Anonymous

Methods Focused on Students

•

Assemble learning activities centred on projects that address actual issues.
Give pupils more control over their work by using choice boards.
Organise student-led debates to foster a sense of ownership over one's learning.
Make use of brainstorming sessions to come up with original concepts.
To keep participants actively engaged, use station rotation.
Create lessons that revolve around what students are interested in.
Establish time for students to reflect on their learning and growth.
Foster teamwork and analytical thinking through the use of peer review.
Get your kids to make a plan for their academic success.
Engage in personal exploration through passion projects.

ಚಿ

"A thoughtful plan turns a class into a community." – Paulo Freire (adapted)

Fostering Originality

Motivate creative problem-solving by participating in brainstorming sessions.
Integrate design-thinking sessions to address creative challenges.
To hone one's narrative abilities, organise storytelling sessions.
Make transdisciplinary lessons more engaging by including music and art.
Encourage self-expression through holding creative writing sessions.
Motivate your pupils to make their animated shorts.
Plan activities for the maker space to encourage practical learning.
Investigate social or historical subjects through role-playing activities.
Arrange contests that emphasise creativity, like app-making or inventions.
Create free-form tasks that give students room to manoeuvre in their completion.

છ

"Preparation shows students you value their time." –
Anonymous

Expanding One's Professional Network

Motivate educators to participate in online communities that share best practices.
For extracurricular activities, form alliances with neighbourhood companies.
Build relationships with universities to gain access to their resources and faculty.
Framework programs for the exchange of teachers between different educational institutions.

"Effective planning saves time and enhances learning." – Linda Darling-Hammond

Gather world-renowned educators for lectures.

Join programs and networks of worldwide educators.
Arrange online seminars, including well-known
teachers.
Form professional learning groups focused on specific
subjects.
Get a feel for current trends worldwide by attending
conferences like ISTE or NEA.
Encourage partnerships with EdTech companies to
create resources.

"A lesson plan is a roadmap to student engagement." – Jay McTighe

To expand perspectives, incorporate global case studies.

Arrange classes that honour the customs and traditions of different cultures.
International exchange programs can help people from different cultures learn from one another.
To teach inclusivity, use literature from various authors.
Make plans for classes covering international problems and group efforts to solve them.
Promote cross-cultural discussions on ethical dilemmas.
Create initiatives centred around the Sustainable Development Goals (SDGs).
Cultural nuances can be taught through language classes.
For transdisciplinary learning, emphasise historical global movements.
Set up exercises like Model UN to hone diplomatic abilities.

℘

"Great teaching begins long before the students arrive." – Anonymous

છ

The Promotion of Social and Emotional Learning

Establish a serene atmosphere conducive to learning by using mindfulness activities.
Create collaborative and empathetic group activities.
Journaling about one's emotions can help.
Engage in role-playing exercises to promote practical conflict-resolution skills.
Make plans to do things that will bring people joy and appreciation.
Discuss moral and ethical challenges through the use of narrative.
Incorporate social bonding initiatives that involve peer mentoring.
Lead community service projects that foster empathy.
Teach decision-making abilities through the use of social contexts.
Add exercises that focus on expressing and using words to describe emotions.

৪৩

"Plans are flexible tools for delivering success." – Carol Dweck

Innovation in Lesson Design: A Journey of Discovery

Work together with coworkers to develop cross-disciplinary initiatives.
Use AI techniques to evaluate and anticipate knowledge gaps.
Make use of 3D printing to educate students about engineering.
Design coding classes that cover a variety of topics.
Use features such as leaderboards and badges to make it more playable.
To promote creative risk-taking, hold "fail-forward" sessions.
Enhance interactive learning with real-time data visualisation.
Arrange design-thinking contests to find workable answers.
Arrange hackathons focused on technology.
Augmented reality can be used to create a more immersive learning experience.

"Thorough planning sets the stage for creative teaching." –
Anonymous

Involvement of Parents and the Community

*Make sure to incorporate parent-student collaboration
into your class preparations.
Arrange meetings to teach parents how to help their
children learn at home.
Gather the local community for career fairs.
To get families involved in displaying their customs,
organise cultural fairs.
Stay informed about the learning goals by sending
out newsletters to parents.
Create materials that can be used to spark
conversations about teachings within families.
"Bring Your Parent to School" events are held on some
days.
Participate in arts and STEM events with your
parents.
Collaborate with nearby businesses to provide
vocational training.
Hold open houses to review the results of the lessons
and the plans for the future.*

ॐ

"Well-planned lessons lead to well-prepared learners." –
Anonymous

Improving Educational Accessibility

Arrange classes per the principles of universally designed learning (UDL).
Students with disabilities should have access to assistive technology.
Make your content more accessible by using plain language and images.
Create exercises that engage several senses to accommodate different ways of learning.
Make sure that videos have transcripts or subtitles.
Lessons can be structured with more leeway for students who study at a slower rate.
Students who are facing difficulties can participate in peer support programs.
To improve inclusiveness, create materials that are both auditory and tactile.
Develop accessible evaluations that are suitable for all learners.
Teach educators how to use adaptive technology to support students with unique needs.

"Planning for students' success is the first step in teaching." – Anonymous

The Importance of Digital Literacy in Curriculum Development

Make plans to teach students to be safe online and recognise signs of cyberbullying.
Make use of online collaboration platforms such as Google Workspace.
Instruct pupils in the art of critical evaluation of internet resources.
For creative project submissions, utilise multimedia platforms.
Make plans with Python or Scratch, two coding environments.
Talk about digital traces and internet morality.
Enhance learning experiences by hosting virtual field trips.
Conduct scientific experiments using virtual labs.
Online tools can be used to teach data visualisation.
Show pupils how AI is being used in their respective fields.

www.authordheerajmehrotra.com

Thoughts on the Methods of Instruction

Keep a journal daily to reflect on how well you're
teaching.
Make use of video recordings to assess student
progress in the classroom.
Maintain a schedule of self-evaluation surveys.
To get helpful criticism, look into peer reviews.
Make better use of future tactics by analysing lesson
results.
Take part in seminars designed to advance your
career.
Gather your coworkers for a conversation after the
class.
Plan lessons with student input in mind.

"Lesson planning is the unsung hero of classroom excellence." – Anonymous

Make use of reflective questions to find out what you don't know.

To gain fresh perspectives, peruse instructional podcasts or blogs.
The seventeenth. Play and Gamification in the Classroom
Create courses that include challenges in the form of escape rooms.
Create quizzes and tests using game-like applications such as Kahoot or Quizizz.
Arrange treasure hunts that are connected to your course material.
Make memorisation games out of card decks.

www.authordheerajmehrotra.com

Investigate literary or historical events with the use of role-playing games.

• 83 •

Incorporate quizzes with a competitive element to encourage participation.
Come up with logical and strategic board games.
Incorporate simulations into the study of science and business.
Create incentive programs to boost engagement.
Make use of gaming platforms to practise solving problems.

"The best teaching moments often stem from the best preparation." – Anonymous

&

Eco-Friendly Curriculum Integration

*To address local ecological concerns, devise projects.
Arrange gardening or recycling events on campus.
Renewable energy sources should be taught.
Explore the implications of climate change through
the use of films.
Establish a schedule for conducting trials aimed at
reducing water use.
As a service learning component, create programs to
clean up your neighbourhood.
Include works on environmental issues in suggested
reading lists.
Incorporate environmental mathematics into
coursework.
Plan outdoor excursions to learn about plant and
animal life.
Collaborate on cross-disciplinary projects focused on
sustainable lifestyles.*

"Preparation creates the foundation for inspired learning." –
Maria Montessori (adapted)

Helping Students Learn Social and Emotional Competencies in the Classroom

Make time every day to practise mindfulness.
To teach empathy, organise role-playing exercises.
Investigate your feelings by keeping a reflective notebook.
Lend literacy classes books that have social and emotional learning aspects.
Guide small-group conversations about settling disputes.
Assist pupils in expressing themselves via creative projects.
Make up situations where you'll have to make decisions.
Come up with events that honour different perspectives and welcome everyone.
Organise sessions where individuals mentor one another.
Every day, take a moment to think and be grateful.

"When plans are thoughtful, students flourish." – Anonymous

Involving Parents in the Process of Lesson Planning

Submit lesson plans to parents for their input using online portals.
Arrange for families to attend preview sessions of the curriculum.
Participate in project-based learning with parent volunteers.
To encourage learning at home, host workshops for parents.
Make newsletters to inform parents about what's happening in class.
Organise open-house events that showcase learning.
Create workbooks that are suitable for the whole family.
Organise projects that students and parents may work on together.
For exceptional guest lectures, consider consulting parents.
Give evaluation instruments to help with at-home practice.

"A good plan saves time and reduces classroom stress." – Harry Wong

A Focus on Analytical Reasoning and Problem Solving

Create classes that incorporate situations of real-world problems.
Incorporate games and riddles into lessons on reasoning.
Explore alternative perspectives through the use of discussion forms.
Include tasks that use design thinking in STEM classes.
To ignite imagination, ask "what if" questions.
Set up simulated trials or UN sessions.
Develop the ability to evaluate sources critically through instruction in research methods.
Arrange group endeavours where resolving issues is the primary focus.
Problems in design that need responses from students.
Incorporate post-problem-solving reflective debriefs.

"Every great lesson starts with a great plan." – Anonymous

Strengthening the Bond Between Educators

• 93 •

Make plans for opportunities to teach together to promote learning across disciplines.
Contribute lesson plans through online collaboration tools.
Set up sessions for brainstorming based on subjects.
Take part in peer evaluations of pedagogical approaches.
During staff meetings, share the best practices.
Collaborate as a team to organise skill-building sessions.
It is highly recommended that educators monitor each other's lessons.
Make sure that all assessments are consistent by creating shared rubrics.
Facilitate cross-grade group initiatives.
Set up retreats where teachers may bond as a team.

"Lesson plans align intention with impact." – Anonymous

Encouraging Environmental Literacy

*Make environmental topics a part of social studies
and science classes.
Arrange educational outings to parks and preserves.
Inspire initiatives that focus on material recycling or
upcycling.
Plan initiatives centred on sustainable energy sources.
Make sure to address the effects of climate change in
your discussions.
Plant trees or tend to gardens by hand.
Take advantage of sustainability-related
documentaries or invited speakers.
Set up energy-saving competitions for the entire
school.
Encourage community collaboration in
environmental projects.
Incorporate meaningful teachings and activities into
your Earth Day celebration.*

"The best teachers are master planners." – Charlotte Danielson

Facilitating Culturally Sensitive Lessons

Include a variety of viewpoints when writing about the past.
Arrange for classroom activities that promote cultural interchange.
For reading assignments, incorporate works from a variety of civilisations.
Incorporate cultural celebrations within the course of study.
Ensure that items suitable for kids who speak more than one language are included.
Ask the presenters to talk about their cultural backgrounds.
Come up with examples that show how the world is interconnected.
Encourage culturally diverse art and music classes.
Dive into different cultures' customs by utilising digital resources.
Use cultural tales to impart moral principles.

"Planning is the secret ingredient to effective teaching." –
Anonymous

Improving Teaching and Learning Executed by Students

●

Give students a chance to lead conferences and share what they've learnt.
Students should be given the freedom to create their assessments.
Utilise student-driven learning through project-based learning.
Incorporate periods of student-to-student instruction into the curriculum.
Form decision-making committees in the classroom.
Arrange for student-led brainstorming sessions.
Provide students with the option to follow personalised lesson plans.
Allow pupils to assess their progress in learning.
Promote entrepreneurship through course projects.
Set up Genius Hour so that kids can pursue their interests.

ಳ

"Prepared teachers create prepared students." – Anonymous

Equipping Students for Professions of the Future

Arrange job fairs that feature representatives from a variety of industries.
Begin teaching the fundamentals of AI and coding to young students.
Create classes that will teach students about budgeting and financial literacy.
Create internship opportunities by partnering with neighbourhood companies.
Work on developing your leadership and teamwork abilities simultaneously.
Invite experts from different domains to provide guest lectures.
Discussions or exercises based on actual business problems can be planned.
Mentor students in the art of persuasion and interview skills.
Put technology to work by simulating problem-solving activities in the workplace.
Create programs that connect students with professionals in their field for the long haul.

ॐ

"A structured plan leads to unstructured creativity." –
Anonymous

Strengthening Subject Collaboration

Create projects that span disciplines, bringing together the arts and sciences.
Work in groups with educators specialising in different areas of study.
Incorporate teachings that connect mathematical ideas to practical economic principles.
Create literature and geography-based history classes.
Incorporate engineering and creative design into STEAM activities.
Emphasise the ability to think critically and apply it across disciplines.
Develop subject-specific evaluation tools like rubrics.
Present integrated learning at multi-subject fairs.
Collaborate on class projects using technological resources.
Encourage cross-disciplinary problem-solving through teamwork.

"Planning creates clarity, clarity creates confidence." –
Anonymous

Fostering Closer Bonds Between Educators and Their Students

Get to know each student's aspirations by scheduling individual encounters.
Gather to honour students' accomplishments, no matter how large or minor.
Make sure that lessons incorporate social-emotional check-ins.
Take the time to listen to them and address their issues.
Make messages more tailored to each student's requirements.
Conduct class activities that foster empathy.
Stay after or during the day to help students who need it.
Research and honour the cultural origins of your pupils.
Promote available avenues for feedback through open communication.
Honour classroom customs and special times spent together.

"A lesson plan is the teacher's compass." – John Dewey (adapted)

Using Gamification to Enhance Lesson Planning

Learn design through completing missions or difficulties in a game.
Make an incentive program to encourage student engagement in class.
Make use of activities that mimic escape rooms to educate students.
Use digital learning games that align with the curriculum's objectives.
Give out awards or badges when they reach specific goals.
Establishing leaderboards can foster a spirit of friendly rivalry.
Make schoolwork more engaging by adding levels.
Introduce new subjects via puzzles or riddles.
Use group activities that involve interactive whiteboards.
Have the class work together to create a game related to their study.

"Good plans create great results." – Anonymous

Highlighting International Viewpoints in Curriculum Development

English classes should incorporate works from throughout the world into their curriculum.
Consider different cultural viewpoints on past events and compare them.
Prepare geography classes that will address global concerns such as climate change.
Immerse students in different cultures to help them learn a new language.
Get people talking about what's happening in the world right now.
Take part in online discussions with classes all over the world.
Include international case studies in business and economics curricula.
Put technology to work by simulating scenario-based global decision-making.
Plan events to commemorate World Heritage Days.
Prompt discussions about problems and potential solutions plaguing the world.

"Invest in planning to invest in success." – Anonymous

Developing Resilience via the Design of Lessons

Lessons should incorporate tactics for a growth mentality.
Tell the tales of historical heroes who triumphed over challenges.
Work through real-world problems to teach problem-solving skills.
As a means of gaining knowledge, talk about setbacks.
Make plans for self-reflection activities that focus on overcoming challenges.
Include tasks that call for teams to work together under time constraints.
Themes of tenacity and persistence can be explored through literature.
Learn how to manage stress with mindfulness exercises.
Exercises, including role-playing, can be used to teach flexibility.
Join students in celebrating significant achievements in resilience.

"Planning is where teaching dreams become reality." – Anonymous

About The Author

Dheeraj Mehrotra, a white and a yellow belt in SIX SIGMA, a Certified NLP Business Diploma holder, is an Educational Innovator, Author with expertise in Six Sigma In Education, Academic Audits, Neuro-Linguistic Programming (NLP), Total Quality Management In Education, an Experiential Educator, a CBSE Resource towards School Assessment (SQAA), CCE, JIT, Five S, and KAIZEN. He has authored over 100 books on computer science, AI, digital body language, NLP, quality circles, school management, classroom effectiveness, and safety and security. A former Principal at De Indian Public School, New Delhi, (INDIA), NPS International School, Guwahati, Kunwar's Global School, Lucknow and an Education Officer at GEMS, Gurgaon, with ample teaching experience of over Three Decades, he is a certified Trainer for Quality Circles/ TQM in Education and QCI Standards for School Accreditation/ School Audits and Management. He has also been honoured with the President of India's National Teacher Award in 2006 and the Best Science Teacher State Award (By the Ministry of Science and Technology, State of UP), among others. He has published over 100 books and developed 150 FREE EDUCATIONAL MOBILE Apps for the Google Play Store exclusively for Teachers, Students, and Parents. This work has been recognised by the LIMCA BOOK OF RECORDS and INDIA BOOK OF RECORDS as the only Indian to draw that feast. As a premium UDEMY Instructor, he has developed over 500 courses and caters to over 8 Lakh students from 180 countries. As a founder and president of the IoT Society of India, he also promotes Technology Globally. Dr Mehrotra is presently engaged as a REGIONAL HEAD of the GEMS EDUCATION India.

www.authordheerajmehrotra.com

BOOKS BY THE SAME AUTHOR